# The Temple Within

## Fellowship with an Indwelling Christ

**Milt Rodriguez**

# Get the Picture?

God loves to communicate to us through the use of pictures and stories. We can easily see throughout the Old Testament how He communicates spiritual truth by using stories, people, animals, and even inanimate objects.

One such "picture" is the *rock* at Horeb that Moses struck with his staff. Paul tells us in the New Testament that this rock was Christ. It provided water for the children of Israel. The rock was a "picture" of Christ who provides us with the living water. Of course, this is just one such example of the way God uses pictures to communicate His Son to us.

I believe this is because of the way He made our minds. An image tends to leave a longer lasting impression on us than an audible message. Sometimes we see an image or a picture and can remember it for months or even years afterwards. However, if we hear a spoken message we will usually forget what was said within a week or even a few days. Somehow, the images stick in our minds longer. I believe the reason that *our* minds work this way is because that's how God's mind works. After all, we were created in

His image, even though that image was marred through the Fall.

God is not primarily a *word* God. What I mean by that is that He thinks and communicates primarily through the use of pictures instead of words. Like they say, "a picture is worth a thousand words." God would rather show us things by giving us pictures than by lengthy spoken explanations.

I know that many of you right now are wondering about the bible. I mean, isn't the bible the Word of God and filled with His words? Yes, of course. But please notice with me that most of those words are used to describe pictures. Let me just point out a few to illustrate my point. The Garden of Eden, the tree of life, the river of life, the tree of the knowledge of good and evil, the man made out of dust, the woman made out of the man, the land of Canaan, the land of Egypt, the lamb that was slain, the desert, the manna, the rock, the stone tablets, the tabernacle, pillar of fire, the cloud, the temple, the people of Israel, the star, the manger, the baby, the shepherd and sheep, the bread, the vine and branches, the wine and wineskin, the door, the way, etc. Of course, we could go on and on with all the pictures in the bible but I think I've made my point.

Our God is a God of revelation. He likes to *reveal* things to us. There is something He wants to show us and He does that by an unveiling or by revealing it to us. You could think of it as a beautiful statue that is behind a veil or a curtain. He opens the curtains very slowly to *show* us more and more of the statue. He *opens* our eyes to *see* things. Of course, we are speaking spiritually here and many times the pictures have to enter our minds before they enter our spirits.

4

Since our spirits are not very developed, God must try to get through to us by giving these pictures to our minds. The mind will hold images longer than anything else. Then, He has a chance to open our spirits to receive the image that is in our mind. Hopefully, we will choose to receive this image and learn to perceive it with our spirits. God reveals the truth behind the picture to our spirits in order for us to understand spiritually instead of just intellectually.

## The Picture of the Temple

The scriptural picture that I will focus on in this book is that of the Temple. This is an image that runs all the way through scripture and can be found, in one form or another, throughout the whole bible.

We will not be so concerned with the picture itself, but rather the reality behind the image. The image reminds us of and points us to the reality. When I see a photograph of my grandchildren, it makes me smile. I smile not because of the photo itself, but because of who the photo brings to my memory. It's the children *themselves* that make me happy. The photo only serves as a reminder or as a sign pointing to the reality.

There is much reality behind the picture of the Temple in both the Old and New Testament. If I could sum up in one phrase the meaning and purpose of the Temple, it would be as follows: *the Temple is the meeting place of God and man.*

There were two problems with this externally based law. First, an external law could never initiate change within the inner man. Something on the outside cannot transform you on the inside. That's trying to work backwards. We can only be changed or transformed from the inside out. It may help to understand this if you think about rotten fruit. An apple always rots from the inside first. When you see rottenness on the outside, then you know that the core is already rotten. Because of the fall, man is rotten to the core. We cannot "fix" this situation. In fact, even God cannot fix this situation! His solution to the fall of man is much more radical than the band-aid approach. Obeying a list of laws will never make you a "good" person. You see, it's not just that the things you *do* are wrong, it's the fact that you, *yourself*, are wrong! It's who you are, your very nature, that is all wrong. A quick fix on the outside will never bring about permanent change on the inside.

The other problem with the external law was that no one could obey it! No one could keep all of the law. When Jesus came, He showed us the full intent of the law. He told us that it wasn't just the outward actions that could not get in line with God's holiness; it was also the intents and motives of the heart. He would quote from the law and then say: "but I say." He told us that even if we are angry with our brother, we have committed murder in our hearts. This proved to us once and for all that none of us could ever fully obey the law. But if you fail to obey one part of the law, then you have failed to obey all of it. There is no one who is good; no not one.

live the Christian life. Yet the bible does not even point to the bible as the means of life. We hear the pastor preach a sermon on Sunday and then we try to do what he says. The scriptures point us to Christ as the means of Life!

Getting to know God means getting to know the bible. We still have God locked up in a box, or should I say a *book*? Please don't misunderstand me here. I am *not* against the bible in any way. I believe it is the written word of God. However, we need to heed the words of Paul concerning this matter.

"For he is not a Jew who is one outwardly; neither is circumcision that which is outward in the flesh. But he is a Jew who is one *inwardly*; and circumcision is that which is of the heart, by the *Spirit*; not by the letter; and his praise is not from men, but from God." Romans 2:28, 29

Here, Paul is describing for us the difference between the Old Covenant and the New Covenant. The old is outward and in the flesh. The new is inward and in the spirit. If we just have the letter (the Scriptures), then that will be religion. We must be in the spirit. The letter by itself kills, but the spirit gives life. Inward life here is the key, not just an outward adherence to a written code.

We view Him as being outside of us up in heaven somewhere. We have no Christ-in-you consciousness. We believe doctrinally that Christ lives in us but we don't live like it. We live a mechanical Christian life based upon our ability to obey the scriptures. None of us can keep the law, why do we think that we can obey all the scriptures? That's not the New Covenant. That's not even feasible! The New Covenant is based upon us living by the life of Another. This other Person lives inside of us. We are to live by His life, not our own.

# The Christ Life

Jesus did not live out His spiritual life like we do today. He did not live by means of external actions or duties. The power of His "Christian" life was not based upon going to church, reading the scrolls, prayer, tithing, or preaching about Himself. The basis for His spiritual life was His internal fellowship with His Father. In fact, He told us that He lived by means of the life of His Father. (John 6:57) He also told us that "the Son can do nothing of Himself." Jesus kept telling us over and over again that it was the Father in Him that was doing the work and speaking the words. He showed us how a man can live by divine life. He showed us by living it out in front of us. He lived by the life of an indwelling Father.

Dear Reader, the goal of this book is to help you come out of living by the Old Covenant and start living by the New Covenant. You have been struggling to live a good "Christian" life for so long, but is it working? Have you not failed miserably at this exactly like the rest of us?

I am here to tell you that failure and frustration are all you will face as long as you try to live by the Old Covenant way. God has a "new" way, a much better way for you to live. Paul called this way "Christ in you, the hope of glory"! Your Lord so greatly desires for you to know this Way. He so much wants you to know Him and fellowship with Him. He so much wants to show you all the riches that are in Christ Jesus!

# Being in Christ

There is so much bounty, so many riches, and so much glory inside of your Lord that it would take all of us the rest of our lives just to begin to describe it all. And even then, it would be done oh so feebly! But it is so important that you and I catch a glimpse; a glimpse of what is inside of Christ. Our Lord is so much greater than we could ever have imagined. He is so much bigger and fuller than we ever thought possible.

I am going to attempt to describe to you just a few of those things that are in Him. It's important that you understand what is in Him so when you discover that He is in you, you will have a fuller comprehension of what *that* means.

First, I am simply going to make a partial list of some of the things that the scriptures tell us are "in Christ."

The Creation is *in* Christ.
The Life is *in* Christ.
The Acceptance is *in* Christ.
The Redemption is *in* Christ.

The Righteousness is *in* Christ.
The Sanctification is *in* Christ.
The Hope is *in* Christ.
The Spiritual Blessings are *in* Christ.
The Consolation is *in* Christ.
The Peace is *in* Christ.
The Effectual Prayer is only *in* Christ.
The Strength and Riches are *in* Christ.
The Eternal Purpose is *in* Christ.
The New Creation is *in* Christ.
The Promises are *in* Christ.
The Escape from Condemnation is *in* Christ.
The One Body is *in* Christ.
The Perseverance is *in* Christ.
The Gathering into One is *in* Christ.
The Bonds of Suffering Believers are *in* Christ.
The "No Separation" is *in* Christ.
The Perfect Man is *in* Christ.
The Helpers Together are *in* Christ.
There are the Churches *in* Christ.
There are the Dead *in* Christ.
There is the One New Man and the Perfect Man *in* Christ.
We are complete *in* Christ.
And there is much, much more . . .

## The Christ "Environment"

If you are a Spirit-born believer, then YOU also are *in* Christ!  This is not just some lofty philosophical or theological theory.  We are not just talking doctrine here.  This is not just some nebulous idea or concept.  This is reality,

You also must be willing to admit that you really don't know the Lord very well at all. After being a Christian for over twenty years, I was at a place where I realized that I didn't really *know* Him in the truest sense of the word. Oh, I knew a lot *about* Him and the scriptures, but I didn't know Him *as a Person who lived inside of me.* I didn't even know Him as well as I knew my wife, and this was a Person who lived inside of me! If you really want this revelation of *Christ in you*, you must ask for it. Paul deliberately went away into Arabia to spend time alone with his Lord. He "ran after" Him with a great fervor. But it was the *Father* who was pleased to reveal His Son in Paul.

Please be aware that revelation always comes at a price. You will definitely be misunderstood when you start telling people that Christ lives in you. Even telling other believers will get you some strange glares! Some may even consider you to now have become a "New Ager" because you are speaking of the "Christ Within." But nothing could be more scriptural, and nothing could be truer.

## The Purpose of an Indwelling Christ

God's intention in the Garden of Eden was for Adam and Eve to eat of the tree of life. He wanted His divine Life to dwell *within* them. Now this tree of life that we see in the garden is a picture of the Lord Jesus Christ. He said, "I am the true Vine (or tree)." He comes to live in us so that we will contain the life of God. But why? Why does God put His life within us?

There are actually two answers to that question. First, God places His life within us because He loves us and wants to have fellowship with us. God wants to be one with man. He wants to have a counterpart or help-meet just like Adam had Eve. In other words, He wants to have a wife! He wants to love her and be loved by her. This is what being the "bride of Christ" is all about. The "two shall become one flesh," translates into; the two shall become one spirit. God has for so long wanted to share His life and love with someone. Now, we are in Christ and He is in us. This makes us one. This is both an individual and corporate matter. God has placed His Son in you so that He could be one with you and have intimate fellowship with you. Since He lives within you, you can come and dine at His table in sweet fellowship at any time and at any place.

The other reason that God has placed His life within you is so that He can be expressed in this realm. God's eternal purpose concerns the fact that God wants to have the *fullness* of His Son expressed in all realms. He wants an "image" of His Son. But this image is not to merely be a clone or carbon copy of His Son. The image is to actually *be* His Son.

When we think of an image we think of a representation of the real thing. For example, a photograph is an "image" of the reality. You take a photograph of a tree and then you can show people what that tree looked like. However, that photograph is not the actual tree. It is just an "image" or representation of the tree. This is *not* the kind of image that God wants. The image that God wants is the *actual* tree seen again here, and there, and everywhere. Christ in you, Christ in me, Christ in us all! It's not that we become *like* Christ, but rather that He is more and more clearly seen in us. We decrease; He increases so that the world can see Him *in us*. God wants to freely express Himself in this physical realm. He wants to be made visible. This is what the term; the *body* of Christ is all about. Paul said that "we have this treasure in earthen vessels."

The third major revelation that Paul received was when he was caught up into the third heaven. He said that he knew a man, *in Christ*, who fourteen years ago was caught up into the third heaven. This answers the third question of "where are you in relationship to Christ"? You are *in Him*!

## Living by the Life of Another

God has placed the resurrected life of His precious Son within *your* ribcage to fulfill an eternal purpose. He wants Christ to be the All in all. He wants every part of this universe to radiate forth with the glory of His Son. You, my friend, are an integral part of this grand purpose. He has placed His Son within you to fulfill and complete your destiny. You are no longer alone and empty. You no longer need to wander aimlessly through this life.

Think about all that is in Christ. Think about all that I shared in the last chapter that is *in* Him. Then, try to apprehend the glorious fact that this magnificent Christ lives *in* you! This is a literal, living reality. God wants to be glorified, and His hope of this glory is that Christ is in you. He cannot accomplish His goal without you and me. It's up to us to choose daily to live by His life or by our own life. It's up to you to yield and give way so that His life can come forth through you.

It all begins with something called "fellowship." The Lord who lives within you wants to fellowship with you on a continual basis. He placed a "temple" within you so that you would have a place, a "house," where you could meet with Him. This divine communion that we call fellowship is where it all began.

This word "fellowship" comes from the Greek word "*koinonia*" which literally means: communion, sharing in common, communication, and partnership. The members of the Godhead were "sharing in common" three main things: their *life*, their *love*, and their *communication.*

## The Life of God

The Father is called the "Father" because all life flows forth from Him. His divine life flows from Him *to* the Son and *through* the Holy Spirit. His life is the essence of who He is. So in other words, He completely gives all of Himself to the Son. This transfer of divine life flows through the "conduit" of the Holy Spirit. God *is* Spirit, so everything that happens in Him, happens in and with Spirit.

The Son receives the life of the Father. He takes that life and then lives by that life. You could say that He "feeds" upon that life. (John 6:57) The Father is the Son's Daily Bread. He continually lives by "feeding" upon the life of His Father. He also returns this same life to the Father. One of the main ingredients of fellowship is *giving*. There is a continual giving away of life that is happening inside of the Godhead. The Father gives away all of His life to the Son and then the Son turns around and gives back all of that life to the Father. The Son gives back the only life He has ever known; the Father's life!

## The Love of God

This divine exchange and interchange of life is happening continually within the temple of God. The giving away of one's life creates another element within this sacred fellowship; divine love! When the Father pours out His life into His beloved Son, then the love of God roars out like a lion.

The Father holds back nothing. He does not reserve a little life for Himself for later. He completely gives His all to the Son. He gives Him everything that He is. Then the Son does the same. He gives the Father everything that He is in return. This total giving, this total sharing, this total communion, this total emptying of one's self for another is the very essence of divine love. The Father does not consider His own loss. The Son does not consider His own loss. The Spirit is the great "exchanger" of this flow of fellowship and does not consider His own loss in this exchange either. The only thought of each Person is for the well being of the other Persons. There is no room for self-centeredness or even self-consciousness here in this fellowship. Each Person in this community of Three is only concerned for the happiness of the others. This loss of life for another is the substance of divine love.

## The Communication of God

Of course, the communication between the members of the Godhead goes much deeper than words. We are speaking of a fellowship that precedes any spoken or written language. *Communication* means to share or exchange ideas and information. The exchange of life and love that happens within this fellowship is much deeper than merely sharing information, to say the least. They are sharing their lives with one another! They are revealing all that They have and all that They are to one another. So this "naked" love is a total unveiling or *revelation* of each of

Their lives to one another. You could say that They communicate through revelation to one another. It's not just a telling, but it's a *showing* or a revealing of all that They are to one another. This total giving, sharing, exchanging of life and love, and communication is the "stuff" that makes up the fellowship of the Godhead.

You may need to stop reading for a while and absorb these things that I have been sharing.

## The Fellowship Continues On Earth

Fellowship is the main activity within the Godhead. Even though the members of the Godhead may engage in other activities, the fellowship is always flowing. It is like a mighty torrential flow of water -- a river that never stops streaming in the heart of God. It is the foundation for everything that God does. It is the foundation for all of His thoughts and all of His plans. Your God is a Community of three Persons. Fellowship is the "glue" that holds that Community together. That fellowship has been going on since before eternity. Everything God does issues forth as a result of that fellowship.

That fellowship was so wonderful and so glorious that it needed to be shared. Total sharing of life and love was (and is) happening within the Community but God wanted to share it outside the Community as well. The Father desired to have more children who would be patterned after His only begotten Son. With this family, He would share His fellowship. The same life, love, and communication would flow within the Godhead to His other sons and daughters. For this reason, He created. For this reason, He sent His beloved Son to the earth.

We can see, if we have eyes to see, the fellowship of the Godhead continue in the earthly life of Jesus of Nazareth. We can see the Father giving Him life, and love, and communicating with Him through the Holy Spirit. The Lord Jesus lived by the life of the Father who dwelled within Him. The Father was *His* Good shepherd. The Father was *His* Manna from heaven. The Father was *His* True Vine and He produced fruit because of the divine life flowing in His veins. The Father was *His* Life and Resurrection. The Father was *His* Door to the other realm. The Father was His All and He could do nothing apart from Him. He continually drew upon His Father's life within Him to do His work. The words He spoke were the Father's words. The works He performed were the Father's works. Even though He could fellowship with the Father all the time, sometimes He needed to withdraw from people so He could be alone with His Father. His Father was calling Him away; away to fellowship together as they had done throughout eternity. This "calling away" was done by and through the Holy Spirit.

We need to see that the fellowship of the Godhead was the foundation and source for everything Jesus did and said. When He spoke, His words did not come from a vacuum. He didn't just pluck those words from out of the air. Everything He said came from deep experience within the Godhead. Everything He did issued forth out of His experience in eternity past from within the fellowship of the divine Community.

When He said, "I am the Bread of life," He was speaking from past experience. He already had a long resume filled with experiences of being and receiving daily bread from within His community. He had already experienced receiving the Father's life as His daily sustenance. He had already experienced giving this "bread" back to the Father and feeding Him with His very own life. He had already experienced the Spirit as His "table" and the one Who would be the conveyor of this life. He knew all about the *Real* bread! He knew what He was talking about. He knew from experience.

It's important that we see that Jesus was not really trying to "teach" us. What He shared with His disciples and with the crowds were not teachings. They were testimonies! He was sharing His own experiences. He was sharing His own experience of *koinonia* from within the community of the Godhead. Before He came to earth, this was His life. This fellowship was everything to Him. He came to earth to expand the fellowship. He came to earth to give this life to us.

**The Temple Comes to Earth**

While here on earth, the Father met with the Lord Jesus in a "secret" place which was hidden away from the eyes of the world. This "temple" was in a place called *spirit*; the human spirit of the Lord Jesus Christ. The meeting place for the Father and Him was inside of His spirit. The temple was now located inside of the Lord's ribcage! The Father, the Son, and the Holy Spirit now met inside of the human spirit of Jesus of Nazareth. The fellowship never stopped. The location of the temple changed but not the substance. The essence was the same; spirit. The Father was dwelling inside of this temple just waiting for Jesus to come to Him so that they could continue their sweet fellowship together. Nothing in this world could effect this fellowship because it existed in another realm altogether. Nothing could hinder or destroy this community because the prying hand of the world could not reach this place. He told the Pharisees that if they tore down the temple that in three days He would raise it up. They were thinking about the physical temple made of stone that was standing before them. They couldn't see that the *real* Temple was standing before them; the *Christ*!

This was the Father's place of refuge. This was His place of rest and quiet. This was His home! The life that Jesus lived was activated and energized by this internal fellowship with His Father. We have, in most part, failed to see this in modern day Christianity. We live out our Christian lives by the "power" of our doctrines, creeds, activities and programs. We live by our knowledge of the bible, or our devotion to certain projects. But how much do we know of an inward fellowship with an indwelling Lord? How well do you know the Christ who lives within you?

Many of us base our knowledge of the Lord upon our knowledge of the scriptures. But what if you had no bible? Do you realize that the early believers had no bibles? Most believers in the first century were illiterate and there were very few copies of the Old Testament scrolls to go around. Usually, the only copy of the Old Testament would be in the town synagogue that is, if the town even had a synagogue. How did the early believers get to know the Lord? Obviously, bible study and memorization were not part of it! Could it be that they learned to fellowship with God the same way that Christ fellowshipped with the Father while on earth? Doesn't it make sense to you that the apostles would have taught them to walk with Christ just as they have seen Him "walk" with His Father? The Lord Jesus

# You Are a Temple

Jesus told the disciples that He was going to prepare a place for them. He told them that His Father's house had many rooms and that He was preparing a place for them. (John 14:2, 3) He wanted them to be where He was. He was not referring to your own personal mansion in the sky! He was saying that He was preparing a place of residence for Himself inside of you. This place is a spiritual temple; a place where you and He could meet on a continual basis. It's very important that you and I realize He has setup His home inside of us and that is the place where we go to have fellowship with Him. But where is that temple located?

## The Breath of Life

The scriptures clearly tell us that man is a tripartite being. That is, you are made up of three parts; spirit, soul, and body. I am not going to attempt to describe these three in great detail, but rather give you some basic principles. Other men before me have done a better job at describing

**The Temple of God**

"Do you not know that you are a temple of God, and that the Spirit of God dwells in you"? I Cor. 3:16

Here Paul gives us a beautiful picture of the believer being a temple of God. He ties in the temple with the believer. The temple was made up of three parts. These three parts coincide with the three parts that make up the believer in the Lord Jesus Christ.

The *outer court* represents man's body because it is outward, and is seen by all and visited by all. It is the way of expression and communication with the outside world. All external and physical actions will be performed here.

The *holy place* represents man's soul. This is the place between the spirit and body where the mind, will, and emotions reside. This is the place of the personality and individual self.

The *holy of holies* is the innermost place and the dwelling place of God. Here, man has intimate communion with God. It represents the spirit of man. The spirit lies beyond man's self-consciousness and above his senses. This is the place where God and man are one.

The availability of light in the temple is also an illustration of how things work in us. The outer court (body) is exposed to the broad daylight and can be seen by all. The holy place (soul) is illumined by the lampstand of seven candlesticks which represents the reasoning and thought life of the soul. The holy of holies (spirit) contains no light whatsoever. This place is dark because there is no sight needed here. The spirit completely operates by faith and not by sight. All insight in this place comes by way of direct revelation from God.

God gives us an order for the three parts of man: spirit, soul, and body (I Thess. 5:23). This is very important because God wants the whole man to be governed in and by his spirit. God's intention is that your spirit be governed by His Holy Spirit, and thus control the soul and body. However, because of the Fall, man's soul was enlarged and the "self" or soul took over the control of man's being. God's transformation process includes the reducing of the soul to the proper size and role, and the enlarging of the spirit to the place of control under the direct headship of the indwelling Christ.

## The Prominence of the Spirit

"God is spirit; and those who worship Him must worship in spirit and truth." (John 4:24)

Your spirit is an organ. Just like your body has a liver, kidneys, heart, etc.; so you have a spirit. It's the part of you that allows for spiritual function. You can only receive revelation from God in your spirit. In fact, you can only truly *know* God in your spirit. All spiritual things must be *apprehended* by the spirit, not just the mind or emotions. We are used to functioning primarily with our souls and not our spirits. But God only communicates to us through and in our spirits. First, we need to understand what happened to us at re-birth.

## Eating of the Tree of Life

When you came to Christ and were born from above,

something miraculous happened inside of you. First of all, let me explain that we are all born with a spirit. That spirit is considered to be dead to God, though it is alive to you. For example, part of the functioning of the spirit is conscience. Every person has a conscience. It is the part of your spirit that instinctively knows right from wrong. No one has to teach you this, you just know it instinctively in your spirit. Your spirit is alive and functioning in part in the areas of conscience and instinct. However, it is not alive regarding communion with God. This type of functioning of the spiritual organ can only take place after being "born" of the Spirit.

When you turn to God through faith in Christ, He places His divine life within your spirit. Christ, through the Holy Spirit, comes to live inside of your spirit. Now His Spirit is one with your spirit. You have done what Adam never did. You have eaten of the Tree of Life! God's own life has now come to dwell within you. You now not only have a spirit, but your spirit contains the very life of God! This life is a Person; the Lord Jesus Christ.

**You Are a Hybrid**

So now there is a part in you that is from the heavenly realm. You are "of the earth," but you are also "of the heavens." It could be said that you are two species in one. You have a part (organ) in you that can function in both realms. You, like the Lord Jesus, are a creature of the heavenly and earthly realms; both at the same time! When your Lord walked the earth He was living in two realms at the same time. He walked in this world and functioned as you and I do regarding matters of this physical existence. But

He also walked in the spiritual realm at the same time. He could "see" and "hear" things that belonged to that spiritual realm just as clearly, if not more, than in this earthly one. His Father was the governing force in that spiritual realm and all things issued forth from Him. The *invisible* Father was being expressed by the *visible* Son. In order for the Son to be the visible image of the Father, He had to be intimately connected to the spiritual realm.

You are also a son of the Father (in Christ) and He wants to express Himself through you. However, He can only do this if you are walking in the spiritual realm as well as the earthly. For this purpose, you are a hybrid of the spiritual and physical realms. This is why learning to function (and live) in your spirit is so important. Paul told the brothers and sisters in the churches he planted to walk and live in their spirits. Please realize that walking in *your* spirit is the same as walking in *His* Spirit because they have become one! The two have become one spirit. Now you and I can walk in two realms at the same time. We can be governed by the heavenly realm and live out the practical expression of that realm in our daily lives here on earth. Christ can be made visible again.

Paul said that he looked at the things which are not seen. The things which are seen *are* only temporary, while the things which are *not* seen are eternal. The problem today is that we focus on the things which are seen. Most of what we call "Christian" comes out of the soul life, not the spirit. We really don't know much at all about how to function in our spirits. Most of our "spirituality" comes from our heads. The soul is still very much in charge, and therefore, we mostly relate to God through our intellects, emotions, and wills. But Jesus told us that God is a Spirit and the only way to relate to Him was through (or in) spirit. You are the temple of God. The holy, living God of this universe dwells inside of you. Your spirit is His throne, resting place, and home. Your spirit is the holy of holies.

Dear believer, are you hungry to know your Lord in spirit and reality? Are you longing to touch Him who lives in the deepest parts of your being? Is your spirit being drawn to Him as you read these words? Are you tired of only knowing Him on a surface level? If you are hungry and desperate to know Him in the depths then let's walk together through the torn veil into the holiest place of all!

"The Christian life as lived out in the Godhead, before the eternals. Yes, even back then you find the Christian life . . . and it was being lived out in the Godhead. Here, at last, is bedrock! Here are the unmovables. Here are constants that never change. Whatever is going on here, you can be sure, foreshadows how you are to live the Christian life. Isn't that wonderful"!

~ Gene Edwards ~

*one* church!  So why would we need a name?

## The Ever Present One

I like the fact that God uses this "I AM" designation. Notice He does not call Himself "I was" or "I will be," He says "I AM."  He *is* right now.  God does not live in time and space.  He is not bound by the confines of this physical realm.  He lives in a place that is both beyond and yet encompasses both past and future.  Since time is *in* Him, He sees *all* of time at once; past, present, and future.  They are all happening *now* to Him.  All is in the present.  He is the Eternal Now; He is the Eternal I AM.  This has everything to do with your fellowship with Him.  The temple that lives within you is *now*.

Knowing this about God helps us to know some-thing about ourselves.  Since we are to live in Him, we are to live in that ever present now, the Eternal Now.  Jesus told us not to worry about tomorrow, but to seek God's kingdom today.  God's kingdom is the place where God lives and that place has this "Eternal Now" quality about it.  That kingdom is within us, within our spirits, and there is no time or space there.  There is only "Now."

## Living in the Moment

Many New Age teachers tell us nowadays that we should live "in the moment."  They tell us that we are too "stressed out" and that's because we are so busy regretting (and having guilt over) the past, and planning and worrying (fear) about the future.  We totally miss enjoying and living in the present because we dwell in the past or live for the future. They also tell us that we need to learn how to "live in the moment," how to make the most of the time we have right now, today, in fact in this very hour! You know; '*carpe diem*', seize the day, live for today, live in the moment.

Now I agree with the basic tenets of this philosophy. However, it's the method that I disagree with. The idea that we need to enjoy the present moment and not dwell on the past or worry about the future is something that Jesus told us in the Gospels. However, He gave us a totally new, revolutionary way of doing that. His "method" solved the two main problems that we run into when we try to live the way that the philosophers of the world suggest.

## Where is Now?

One of the problems is the fact that working hard at living "in the moment" just becomes another point of stress in our lives! We are trying to relieve the stress by enjoying today, however, now we have to learn a new skill; living in the moment. That just serves to add more stress into our lives especially when we fail and then feel guilty about our failure! Now we are once again caught in the trap of regretting the past and worrying about the future. Now, we worry about how we are going to handle our next opportunity to live "in the moment."

The second problem we have is actually an explanation for the first problem. Is it even possible to totally live in the *now*? As creatures trapped within this cage we call "time," is it even possible to experience the "now"? I am not trying to wax philosophical or even scientific here. My question is this; is there such a thing as the true "now" or "present"? We could say that the concept is that the *present* is the gap of time between the *future* and the *past*. Would you not agree with that? The question is – does such a gap even exist? Isn't it true that the moment the future comes to us, it has become the past? Let me illustrate.

When I speak the word "present," the moment that I speak it, it has become part of the past. This is a good example because I can *think* the word before I *speak* it. Just to illustrate, we could say that when we think of the word we know it is going to happen "in the future." Obviously, we *think* the word "present" before we actually *speak* it. However, the moment we speak it, the word enters into the past.

Let's imagine for a moment that past and future are two adjoining rooms. Past is a room and Future is a connected room. The only thing separating the two rooms is a doorway. Segments of time pass from one room to another with very little (if any) time in between. You can (mentally or emotionally) live in one room or the other; however, you cannot live in the doorway. There just isn't enough "room" there!

## Is There an Escape from Time?

So we could accurately say that within the confines of time, there really is no true "present" or "now" as far as we are concerned. If the "present" does exist within time (which I don't think it does), then it is definitely too small a space for us to live in because it is only the *portal* between past and future.

So where do we find the true "now"? Is there any escape from this prison of past/future dichotomy within which we live? Is it possible to enter a third "dimension" that we normally call "the present" or "the Now"? Could such a place exist where the chains of past and future no longer have any hold on us? Could such a place of unbridled freedom really exist?

## The Kingdom Within

Yes, this place does definitely exist and the Lord Jesus spent most of His time here on earth trying to tell us about it. However, this place does not exist within time at all! It exists outside of space and time and inside of the One who called Himself; "I AM." It is now the time to learn how to take Christ as our *Eternal Now*.

## The Father's House

"Let not your heart be troubled; believe in God, believe also in Me. In My father's house are many dwelling places; if it were not so, I would have told you; for I go to prepare a place for you. And if I go and prepare a place for you, I will come again, and receive you to Myself; that where *I am*, there you may be also." John 14:1-3

We seem to be trapped within the past and future and the closest we can get to living "in the moment" is actually living in the recent past. However, if we were able to travel outside of time and then into the One who called Himself the "I AM" then we could actually experience this thing we call the "now." Whether you are a believer or not, I propose to you that you are looking in the wrong place for this experience of living in the moment. That cannot happen here. It can only happen in a different place. It can only happen in a place that Jesus said He would go to prepare for us; a place where we could go to behold Him and be with Him and experience Him as the great "I AM."

What and where is the Father's house? I realize that when most of us read this passage in John 14 about the Father's house we get this picture in our minds of this palace or castle floating among the clouds up there in the upper atmosphere. There are these mansions floating up there that are just waiting for us to come and inhabit once we die and go to "heaven." But is this really what Jesus was talking about? We have already seen that the place He was referring to is the "house" or temple within your spirit. This is a place without space or time. This is a place inside of the living Christ! The Father's house is inside of His dear Son! *That* is the place where we can find the *Eternal Now*. That is the place where we can be free from the tyranny of time. That is the place where we can discover the glorious "I AM"!

Dear reader, Eternity lives inside of you. You can live in that place of eternal now, you can live "in the moment" by living inside of Him. There are no limits to the depths within Him. His increase is without measure and His riches are unsearchable. Plunge yourself into Christ. Sink deep into all that He is. Allow every part of Him to fully saturate every part of you. Close your eyes right now and lose yourself inside of the great "I AM." Let your spirit sink deep into the timeless ocean of the All.

"When you see your thoughts wandering, call yourself back to the present moment, but do not struggle with your thoughts. Just stay in the present and you will soon notice your Lord by your side again. The more you turn back to Him just as soon as you sense yourself wandering, the sooner you will have the blessing of knowing the indwelling presence of Christ in a more constant and familiar way."

~ Francois Fenelon ~

# Turning to Him

## The Act of Fellowship

Every true believer has the living Christ dwelling within his spirit. However, most of us never really learn to fellowship with Him there in our inward temple. Just because He is there doesn't mean that we commune with Him. We have the Bread of Life dwelling inside of us and yet our spirits are starving to death! Obviously, just having the food isn't good enough. You must actually rise up and eat. This takes conscious effort on your part. *You* must take the initiative, become a participant, and eat.

In John 15, the Lord tells us that He is the true (real) vine and we are the branches. Then He tells us to "abide" in Him. Isn't that strange? The "tree" is telling the "branches" to abide in Him. What else would branches do but abide in the vine? Apparently, this "abiding" that He is speaking of is something more involved than the branches just being "stuck" on the vine. You and I are in Christ, but are we *abiding* in Christ? You see, being *in Christ* is a position whereas *abiding* in Christ is an activity. The position gives us the ability and opportunity to engage in the activity. However, most Christians never learn to *abide* in Christ. Most believers never learn to *eat* of Christ, even though the very Bread of Life is living within them. This is a very sad situation and one that we hope to help remedy.

**What is the Food?**

First, we need to realize and be able to recognize true food when we see it. What is spiritual food? The preachers tell us that the scriptures and the teaching of the scriptures is our spiritual food. Many Christians view the church as a feeding station or restaurant that they need to attend each week so that they can be spiritually fed. But do the scriptures themselves teach us this? No, they do not. The bible is *not* the bread of life. The bible points us to the food, however. In John 6, Jesus tells us that *He* is the true bread that came out of heaven. He said, "I AM the Bread of Life." You see spiritual food is not a book, or words on a page. True spiritual food is a Person! The bible never points us to the bible. The scriptures always point us to Christ.

This is something that can only be revealed to us by our Father in heaven. The only true food is Christ Himself. He told us that if we eat His flesh and drink His blood we would have life within ourselves. If we would partake of Christ Himself, then we would be able to live by His life, instead of our own human lives.

**Where is the Food?**

We should already know the answer to this question. The Food is within you! Christ, by His Spirit, lives within

## The Center of All Things

Jeanne Guyon used a wonderful illustration to explain how this works. In nature, the center of an object exerts a powerful drawing force. This can be seen clearly in the gravitational pull of the earth's core. If you drop an object, it just quite effortlessly falls to the ground. This is because of gravity: the force of the center of the earth pulling it down. Your Lord lives in the very center or core of your being. He is like a magnet that is drawing you toward Himself.

Another example is water. Water does not need to work in order to run downhill. It just happens effortlessly because of the drawing power of gravity. However, that will not happen if there is something in the way blocking the flow of water from reaching its destination. Remove the obstacles and the water will flow effortlessly.

## The Obstacle of the Mind

The main obstacle you will face as you turn inward to the Lord is your mind. The mind is like a whirlwind. It is constantly active and wandering. The mind, like the tongue, is an unruly member that is difficult to tame. In fact, only the Lord can tame the mind *and* the tongue. You do not need to exert all your effort in trying to control your mind. The only thing you need to do is *turn* your mind to your Lord who is within. This is not mind control. This is not meditation, visualization, or contemplation. I'm speaking of calming your mind by *turning it towards your Lord*.

The bible tells us that as a man *thinks*, so is he. Paul

also tells us to take every thought captive to the obedience of Christ. He also tells us to set our minds on things above, not on things on the earth. That's because he wants us to be able to see the unseen. He wants us to be able to see things from God's perspective, instead of just our own. We are seated with Christ in the heavenly places. Our minds should be in the same place. However, your mind is fallen and by nature tends to dwell on the earthly things. Your mind is easily distracted and constantly pulling you away from the Lord by its many wanderings. However, by God's grace, you can learn to pull your mind back to the Center of your being. You can learn to dwell in the temple within.

Do not force or struggle with your mind. Only continue to turn your thoughts to the indwelling Christ. Do not attempt to conjure up specific thoughts *about* the Lord. Just give Him your attention! Just *turn* to Him. As you give Him all of your attention *He* will commune with you. *He* will take it to the next level. He will lead you by the hand into the holy of holies where you will dine with Him.

Him.  Your mind is like a little child trying to reach something on top of the refrigerator.  It is simply too high and too far to reach.  However, your spirit can grasp these things because there is no such thing as "too high" in the spiritual realm.

## Calming the Mind

We know that Christ Himself is our peace.  He said that if we come to Him, He would give us rest for our souls.  He also told us to *be still* in order to know Him.  But what does it mean to *be still*?  Certainly it means more than just to sit still physically without any bodily movements.  Certainly it means more than when a parent tells a child to be still.  It is your *mind* that needs to be still.  It is just like that hyper-active child who is constantly moving and constantly chattering.  Do you want to discover how "spiritual" you really are?  Just try this simple experiment.  Sit still and quiet and focus all of your thoughts upon Christ for the next five minutes.  Please try this right now.  Put this book down and try pulling all your thoughts to your Lord for the next five minutes.

Well, how did it go?  Was Christ your only thought for the whole five minutes?  Yeah, right!  If you went more than thirty seconds without a distracting thought than you did really well!  As you can see, you and I are not very spiritual people.  Your mind is constantly wandering all over the place and it is not easy to get it to settle down.  This is probably the greatest hindrance to you flowing back to your Center who is Christ.

But be encouraged!  God wants this much more than you do and He is willing to go to great lengths to remove all hindrances to the fellowship He desires to have with you. But there is a part for you to play in all this. He does want you to pursue Him. He does want you to "run" after Him and draw near to Him. He will do the work, but He does expect a small step of faith from you. This "step" of faith is what I call *turning* to Him who is within. Entering into your inner sanctuary where He lives. The first part of this "entering" involves calming your mind and then *turning* all that you are to Him.

**The First Step**

To begin this fellowship in the temple within, it is very important that you find a quiet time and place. As far as possible, you will want to keep all distractions to a minimum. Since the mind will feed on these distractions and pull you away from your Lord, you will want to avoid them as much as possible. Find a quiet time. For most people this will be early in the morning or late at night when everyone else is asleep. Find a quiet, private place. I suggest, to begin with, a quiet room in a building rather than outside. This is because indoors you can have more control over the environment and can keep the distractions to a minimum. You can always go outdoors later after you get some experience in this inward fellowship.

Now just sit and be still before your Lord. Do not pray, do not speak, do not praise, do not read the scriptures. Do not meditate or ponder on a portion of scriptures. Do not try and use your imagination to "visualize" the Lord or anything like that. Just sit and be still before Him. Now, by faith, pull your mind away from all other thoughts to the center of your being. Take your mind by the hand and lead it down into your spirit where your Lord lives. This is done by an act of your will in faith. Your will is leading your mind and emotions to your inward temple to meet with the Lord of all glory. This is done gently, quietly, and reverently. You are pushing aside the veil to enter into the holy of holies. Your Lord is waiting there for you. He is waiting to have sweet fellowship with you. He is waiting to dine with you at His table of love.

## The Importance of Stillness

In order for you to learn how to function in your spirit, it is very important that you learn to quiet down the faculties of your soul. A division of soul and spirit must take place but that can only happen through *His* Spirit. As you quiet your mind, will, and emotions, you are giving Him opportunity to do His work of stirring your spirit to commune with Him. Remember, He lives in the center of your being. He resides in the very core of your spirit.

Sitting quietly before Him is very important because you are ceasing from all your own self-efforts. You are learning to "rest in Him." Deep calls unto deep. His Spirit will call unto your spirit. This takes place in the depths and what takes place in the depths is always silent. The deeper you go, the quieter it becomes. When you are flowing in the oneness of His fellowship you will lose all self awareness. He will become everything and you will be swallowed up in the vastness of His "ocean." In the depths of silence, that is where He will commune with you. That is where He will speak to you. Any revelation or communication will be "stored" in your spirit and will be brought out and revealed to the mind at a later time.

The more that you "eat" of the Lord, that is, the more that you take Him into your spirit, the more you will "see" of Him. "*Taste* and *see* that the Lord is good." Tasting, then seeing. Revelation will pour into your life the more that you partake of Him in your spirit. This "tasting" happens within the quiet stillness of your inner temple.

The battle will take place over this quiet sanctuary of the spirit. *This* is the place of eternal peace. *This* is the place of rest for your soul. *This* is the place of refuge and retreat from the constant noise and activity of the outer world. *This* place is in the very heart of your Lord! He is your sanctuary. He is your peace and your rest. He is your refuge. You must learn to run into Him and be still there. This will not be easy at first and there will be many obstacles.

## How to Handle Distractions

You will find that your mind will begin to wander. It will also take advantage of any outward distractions that occur and will immediately focus on those things. That's alright. As soon as you realize that your mind has wandered away from Christ, gently pull it back to your Lord who is within your innermost being. Do not become distracted with the distractions! What I mean is, do not focus on the fact that you have allowed yourself to become distracted. Just simply turn your soul back to the Lord. Every time your mind wanders pull it back to your Center. Do not wrestle with the distractions. Just turn again to the Lord within. Your spirit knows how to do this. Just let your spirit take charge.

"What is prayer? It is an ascent of the mind to God. He is above us all, and we cannot see Him, therefore we converse with Him. Such prayer as this is the simplest form of prayer. But this is a kind of prayer that is essentially only a mental discourse with God.

"But when the believer fixes his attention on the face of his Lord without requiring consideration, reasoning, without need of proofs to be convinced of anything, this is a higher prayer.

"There is a view of your Lord in which reason, meditation and thought do not play a large part. In the first kind of prayer, one thinks upon God; in the other, one *beholds* Him. The second is a purer practice."

~ Michael Molinos ~

# Beholding Him

After you turn your mind, will, and emotions to the Lord within, then what happens? Then you *behold* Him. There needs to be some explanation here because the word "behold" is not something we use in our day. The word is pregnant with meaning. It means so much more than just *looking* at something or someone.

"Father, I desire that they also, whom Thou hast given Me, be with Me where I am, in order that they may behold My glory, which Thou hast given Me; for Thou didst love Me before the foundations of the world." John 17:24

Do you see the progression here? First, the Lord Jesus asks the Father that we would *be* with Him *where* He is. But where is He? He is in our spirit. The first step is to turn to Him who is in your spirit. The *reason* that we are to turn there is so that we can *behold* His glory. We turn, and then we behold. But what is this mysterious term *"behold"* all about?

According to *Vines Expository Dictionary of New Testament Words*, it means "to look at a thing with special interest and for a purpose, usually indicating the careful to "*behold* the Man"! Beholding Him brings you into participation with the power of His resurrection and the fellowship of His sufferings. Beholding Him will transform you and me into His image. "But we all, with unveiled face *beholding* as in a mirror the glory of the Lord, are being transformed into the same image from glory to glory, just as from the Lord, the Spirit." II Cor. 3:18

## The God of Revelation

As I said before, beholding Him is much more than just looking at Him. It is an actual participation in Christ. When we behold Him, we are partaking of Him. We are eating of the true Bread of Life. It is a good thing to "eat with your eyes"! When we behold Him, He becomes our one true passion and our one true "obsession." The Father is continually beholding the Son and the Son is continually beholding the Father. You could rightly say that the Father only has eyes for the Son and the Son only has eyes for the Father. The Bride only has eyes for her Bridegroom. When she sees Him, her heart leaps within her chest and all her love goes out to her lover. When their eyes meet their spirits become one and true fellowship (community) begins.

We come to know God in a completely different way than we know anything else. We do not *learn* Christ by studying facts about His earthly life or memorizing the red letters in the New Testament. We can only come to know Him intimately when He allows us to really *see* Him. In other words, we come to know Him little by little as He reveals Himself to us. He doesn't "teach" us in the same way we learn in school. We learn by seeing. He instructs us by *showing* us more of Himself. He is a God who is continually unveiling Himself to us. As we are able to receive it, He reveals more and more. *Seeing* really *is* believing!

Paul prayed that God would give the saints a spirit of wisdom and revelation in the knowledge of Him; that the eyes of their hearts would be enlightened. That word for knowledge is *"epiginosis"* which means an intimate knowledge that only comes through direct, personal contact with someone -- a knowledge that comes through intimate experience. The eyes of our spirits must be opened to see Him and His glory. Then, we can truly partake of Him at His banquet table.

**Turn Your Eyes Upon Jesus**

When you turn to Him, it means that you turn your eyes upon Him. This is something which is difficult to explain. You turn the full attention of your soul (mind, will, and emotions) to Him who lives deep inside. Then you turn the eyes of your spirit to Him in all His glory. You do this by an act of your will, in faith. You may or may not sense anything happening in your soul. Most of the time, you will probably not be touched emotionally or intellectually. But there will be times when you come to Him and can't help but weep in His presence. There will be other times when He will give you spiritual insight that will quicken your mind so that it may be able to communicate these "visions." But you need to realize that just because you *don't* sense anything in your soul doesn't mean that nothing is happening. You cannot enter into His temple and behold His glory without an impartation taking place in your spirit. Your spirit *will* be fed and will grow stronger. He *will*

holy writings point to Him. They all concern Him, and they *all* reveal Him. The Old and New Testaments are there as a unified testimony to point us to Christ. This is not an instruction manual to teach us how to live. This is the written revelation of Jesus Christ! It's all about Him. We do not need an instruction manual to show us how to live a good Christian life because we do not live the Christian life. He *is* that Life within us! (Gal. 2:20) We just need to be able to see and touch Him. He is the point of it all.

Secondly, He will *open* the Scriptures to us. You can think of it as a beautiful treasure chest. The scriptures are the "chest" that hold the treasure inside. He must *open* the chest for us to be able to see the glorious treasures inside. The purpose of the chest is to hold the treasure. He *is* the treasure! This *opening* of the scriptures can only happen when the Holy Spirit (who lives in you) reveals Christ to your spirit.

The scriptures should always be used to bring us to Christ. When you start practicing this "art" of beholding Him, you will be able to *behold* Him in the scriptures. Even passages that don't seem to directly relate to Him will come alive with visions of your Lord. He is like a beautiful cut diamond. The scriptures will allow you to see His many angles and the light will reflect in many different colors through that diamond.

You can use the scriptures as a "springboard" to fellowship with the Lord. Take a small passage and read it slowly as if you were savoring a sweet piece of fruit. Taste every aspect of it and allow the writings to bring you to an awareness of your Lord. Let it lead you directly into the holy of holies within your spirit where your Lord is waiting to dine with you.

means *real*, or *genuine*. It contrasts realities with their sem-blances. So Jesus was telling us here that He is the *real* vine and that the created vine that we see is just a picture of Him. He is the reality that was used as a "model" when the vine was created. He is the *real* thing! He also said this about water, a grain of wheat, bread, and many other things.

If we have eyes to see, we can see Him in all of creation. When you develop your sense of spiritual sight, you will begin to see your Lord in many ways and in many things. I'm not saying that those "things" *are* Him, but they are an image or picture of Him. For those who can *see*, these images will point you to Christ. For example, when you look up at the sky at night do you see the moon (an object orbiting the earth), or do you see a picture of the Real Moon? The real Moon is Christ. He perfectly reflects the light and glory of His Father.

Why not take the time right now to behold your Lord? Put down this book, sit back and close your eyes, then turn your soul inward toward your spirit. *Fix* the eyes of your spirit on Him. Take in all of His glory. See Him for who He is. Behold the Lord of glory!

"This King, who is full of goodness and mercy, doesn't punish me. Rather, He embraces me lovingly and invites me to eat at His table. He serves me Himself and gives me the keys to His treasury, treating me as His favorite. He converses with me without mentioning my sins or my forgiveness. My former habits are seemingly forgotten. Although I beg Him to do whatever He wishes with me, He does nothing but caress me. This is what being in His holy presence is like."

~ Brother Lawrence ~

# Loving Him

God created Adam out of the dust of the earth. The word "Adam" means red clay. Adam's body was literally made out of the clay of the earth. However, He did not create Eve out of the red clay, but rather took her from out of Adam. She was called "woman" because she was taken "out of" man. Have you ever wondered why God did it this way? Why didn't He just create Eve out of the dust of the earth like He did Adam? Why did He open up the side of Adam, take out one of his bones, and then create Eve out of that? Isn't this a rather strange way of doing things? Why would He do this? Let me give you a little hint. Remember what we discovered in the last chapter about beholding Him in the scriptures? All of scripture speaks of *Him*.

Adam and Eve are a picture of something else. Paul tells us what that "something" is in Ephesians chapter 5.

"For this cause a man shall leave his father and mother, and shall cleave to his wife; and the two shall become one flesh.

Now, we have already seen that within the fellowship of the Godhead there is an exchange and interchange of divine love. The Father loves the Son with great passion and gives all of His love all of the time to His Son. The Holy Spirit takes the love of the Father and "conveys" this love over to the Son. The Son then (through the Spirit) returns that love back to the Father.

Though this torrential flow of divine love is very satisfying to God, the giving of love could not stop there. This great love had to expand and flow to another "object" outside of God Himself. This is what motivated your God to create. This is what motivated Him to come up with the idea that there could be "another." There could be an "Isshah." There could be a she! God could actually have His own beloved.

God began to put His plan into effect so that He could have His own helpmeet. He created a being who was capable of loving Him just as He loved this being. This creature would also need to have a free will so that she could voluntarily love God since the very nature of love demands that it always be given voluntarily. Love could not be forced or demanded. Yet the only love that would satisfy the heart of God would be His own divine love.

The object of the Father's love is His own beloved Son. He is the *Beloved* of the Father. All of the love of the Father flows out to the Son. The Son returns this love back to the Father and God is very satisfied. However, the Father wanted to expand this fellowship with His Son. He came up with an ingenious plan to actually expand this fellowship by "enlarging" the Son. This would be accomplished by giving birth to many sons within the one Son. They would *all* love Him the same as the one Son because they would

# Does God Have a Need?

All God has ever really wanted was someone to love Him. He has given everything to this end. He is continually pouring out His love to you. He has shed forth His love within you. He has given you everything by giving you Himself. He has given you the ability to love Him by giving you His life. Now He is waiting for two things to happen inside of you. He is waiting for you to *receive* His love, and He is waiting for you to *return* that same love back to Him.

## The Act of Love

There is something that we have missed about our God; He is very romantic. We can see this throughout the scriptures. In many places, He uses very romantic language to communicate with Israel, and later on, with the church. He is definitely a Lover, and because we have missed this point, we have misunderstood many things He has said.

In every marriage there is an act of love. The husband and wife love one another all of the time, but there is a specific act which is an expression of this love. I am referring to what we call the "making of love." The two shall become one flesh. This is a picture of our marriage union with Christ, an expression of the two being one. God loves to be one with us! And there is an act when we come and love Him just as He loves us.

This act is expressed with a word in the New Testament. This word has been greatly misunderstood by believers because of our warped view of God Himself. In many cases, we view God as a high and holy God to be

God wants! He wants you to lose yourself in Him. It's only as you totally give yourself over to Him that your *real* self will be found. You will be found *in Christ*. You must trust Him in this. Give Him all your fears and allow yourself to completely "sink" into His love. He will envelope you, surround you, and even drown you in His love. Receive it. Receive all that He has to give into your spirit and your ability to receive will increase. He will enlarge your capacity to receive as He enlarges your spirit. He will increase and you will decrease inside of your spirit. Fear not little one because He is in you and He will never leave you or forsake you. Allow His love to pour into your spirit, then your soul, then your body. He is knocking, but you must open the door of your heart and allow His glorious love to enter in and fill you up to overflowing. Why not take a few minutes right now to receive His love? Just sit back, close your eyes, quiet your mind, and by faith, begin to allow His love to flow into your spirit.

**Returning His Love**

For many of you, learning to receive His love will take some practice. You may need to sit quietly before Him and just allow yourself to receive His love several times a day before you sense a release in your spirit. Don't be discouraged and don't give up. You will make progress as long as you are consistent.

Of course, *receiving* His love is only one side of the coin. The more important side and the whole reason you need to receive is so that you can give away this great love. Love must always be given away or it is not really love. Love is given to you so that you may give it away. This

"Lastly, a believer who abides within the inmost portion of his being (within his spirit) lives in unbroken peace. Surely there may be outward combats, but the peace is not broken. There is an infinite distance between that inner place and the external tempest; the externals simply cannot reach this heavenly place. The believer can find himself even forsaken, opposed and desolate, but such a storm can only threaten and rage *without*. It has no power within."

~ Michael Molinos ~

# Quality Time in the Temple

You will need to have special times on a daily basis when you can be alone with God. These should be times when outward distractions are at a minimum; you can be alone and quiet before your Lord. It should be at a time and place when/where you will not be disturbed.

## The Place

In our house, we have set aside one bedroom to be used as the "quiet room." It's a small room that only has a few chairs in it. The main reason for the room is to fellowship with the Lord, though it can also be used for reading or another "quiet" activity that requires few distractions and seclusion. When the door is closed to that room, everyone in the house knows that someone is using the room and does not want to be disturbed. Sometimes, I don't want to use that room so I will go outside and find a solitary place instead. It doesn't really matter *where* you go, as long as the place is solitary, in other words, a place where you can get alone with the Lord.

to work during the early morning. That's alright, whenever you wake up, that's *your* morning and you can still start your day with a time of fellowship with the Lord. The idea is to *start* with Him!

Of course, the Lord wants you to *abide* in Him throughout the whole day. But that awaits discussion in another chapter. First, you must establish a "beachhead," a place of beginning from where you can branch out into the rest of your day. Your special quiet time in the morning will set the tone and lay the foundation for your fellowship with the Lord throughout the day. Let's start at the beginning, shall we?

## Some Practical Help

My goal in this chapter is to give you as much practical help as possible without giving you a formula or a method. Please keep in mind that this little "project" is just to be used as a temporary tool to help you get started. Don't make this into a rigid formula! I realize that it may be difficult for many of you to begin right off without any practical direction of any kind. Therefore, I'm suggesting the following project to help you get started. Again, this is not meant to be taken as a "formula" to be used repeatedly in a mechanical way to enter into your inward temple.

## Using Scripture to Enter In

In this project you will use a passage of scripture as a "springboard" to enter into the holy of holies within your spirit. You will want to bring your bible and then get into

**Praying the Scriptures**

In this project you will take a portion of scripture and turn it into personal prayer to the Lord. Then that prayer will be your "springboard" or jumping off place to bring you into the temple of your spirit.

First, turn to the gospel of John and read chapter 6 verses 48 through 58. Read it out loud and slowly. Endeavor to "taste" the Lord in this passage. Savor the meaning of each verse and allow revelation to burst upon you as you read the Lord's words. Do exactly what this passage is talking about and "feast" upon the Lord Jesus Christ. Don't just read the words: taste them, digest them. Those words are the Lord Himself, so take Him in and enjoy every morsel. Don't rush through it. If you sense anything happening in your spirit, pause for a moment and just sit before Him and digest who He is. Then move on to the next portion of scripture.

Once you have completely read this passage then go back and read it again except this time you are going to turn the passage into a prayer to the Lord. Let me give you just one example of how this could be done.

"Lord Jesus, you are my daily food. You are the substance of my sustenance. You are my nourishment, my source of life, and source of everything. You came out of the heavenly realm from the Father to give me this life. You are the true manna that came out of heaven. You are the true bread that feeds my spirit. I now receive You as my food and drink. I take You in and digest You and consume all that You are. I bask in Your love and I drown in our oneness. I love you, Lord, with all that I am. Fill me with all that You are."

lost in Their fellowship with one another. Behold Their fellowship and then allow your spirit to participate in Their fellowship. Love the Father as He loves the Son. Love the Son as He loves the Father. Receive the Father's life from the Son through the Holy Spirit.

Use the rest of your time together to fellowship and love Him quietly. Sit and just be with Him.

The purpose of these three little projects is to show you just three ways that you can use the scriptures to help you enter into His presence. This is to be taken in the context of your special "quiet time" with the Lord in the morning. These special times with Him will be the foundation for the rest of your walk with the Lord throughout the remainder of the day. Try to set aside time in the morning each day; even if you just start with ten minutes a day. The point is to begin! The more you fellowship with Him, the more you will *want* to fellowship with Him.

Please understand that it will take time to develop this relationship with your Lord. It will take time to get to know Him intimately and inwardly. Of course, your inner walk with the Lord will grow and mature as you are consistent in fellowshipping with Him everyday. The key is to begin; and then to be consistent. Even if you only spend a few quality minutes with Him every morning, that's a start.

I also recommend that you begin this inner walk with at least one other believer if at all possible. That way, you can encourage one another. You can also meet together sometimes to be with the Lord. The "exercises" that I give in this chapter can also be done with two or three saints together. For example, when you pray the scriptures, you can take turns praying different parts of the passage and even "bounce" off one another's prayers. As someone

"One question now to be put to the test is this: Can we have that contact with God all the time?  All the time awake, fall asleep in His arms, and awaken in His presence?  Can we attain that?  Can we do His will all the time?  Can we think His thoughts all the time?"

~ Frank Laubach ~

# Habitual Fellowship in the Temple

There are some scriptures pertaining to this that have always intrigued me.

"And Enoch walked [in habitual fellowship] with God; and he was not, for God took him." Genesis 5:24 (Amp.)

"Noah was a just and righteous man, blameless in his [evil] generation; Noah walked [in habitual fellowship] with God." Genesis 6:9 (Amp.)

"But I say, walk and live habitually in the Holy Spirit – responsive to and controlled and guided by the Spirit; then you will certainly not gratify the cravings and desires of the flesh – of human nature without God." Galatians 5:16 (Amp.)

". . . pray without ceasing"; I Thessalonians 5:17

It would seem that the scriptures have answered

get the point. The problem is that we don't get the aware-ness! We all know that God is with us and in us all the time; it's just that we are not consciously aware of that reality as we go about living our daily lives. It's only a theory to us. We do not put this truth into practice.

When I was a young Christian I had read about Noah and Enoch walking in this "habitual" fellowship with God. This was something that I really wanted and decided to make it a goal of my life. I had no idea that thirty years later I would still be struggling with this! Though I have grown and made advances in this walk, it is painfully obvious that I have a long way to go. If you think this is easy, then you are in for a shocker! I don't know of anyone, personally, that walks in a continuous awareness of God's presence. And the awareness is just the first step!

Now of course your fellowship with Him is going to be different as you go about your daily activities. It will differ from your "special" times alone with Him. Normally, I would say that the moment-by-moment walk will be less intense than the "set apart" times. It will be more of an awareness of Him taking place in the background, or deeper within you, as you take care of other activities in the fore-ground. But this may not always be the case.

Right now as I write this chapter, there is a good example of an exception to this. In my "special" times with the Lord, I am struggling right now. I get with Him every morning and yet it is difficult to enter into the holy of holies. I sit before Him yet I don't really ever enter into a sense of His presence. My mind is constantly wandering and I find myself only really focusing on Him a few times during our time together. However, He is meeting with me at the most unexpected times and places throughout the day! I belong to a health spa and I usually go there to work out in the

you mature in this walk.

## Do This in Remembrance of Me

Jesus said that the Holy Spirit would come and dwell in us. He said that the Spirit would remind us of Him. That is, the Holy Spirit would remind us of Christ who lives within us. I believe the Spirit is always attempting to bring our attention to Christ but that we usually don't hear Him because we are so spiritually dull. Sometimes He breaks through all of our self absorption and preoccupied minds and we are reminded that there is a God inside of us who is awaiting our fellowship. So, really, the solution is that we must become more spiritually minded. Some believers say that it is not good to become so heavenly minded that one is no earthly good. Disregard that advice! God wants a nation of people who are so heavenly minded that they *can* actually do some earthly good! Remember, "on earth as it is in heaven"?

Paul told us to set our minds on things above, not on things on the earth (Col. 3:2). The bible calls this the renewing of the mind. As you seek to know the Lord in a deeper way, more and more of your thoughts will turn to Him. You will begin to see Him in everything and in every place and situation. This is the "beholding" that we talked about previously. You will begin to be able to hear the Holy Spirit reminding you of His presence so that you can turn to Him in your spirit. It may be just a brief turning to Him but this can take place all throughout the day.

What do you think Jesus was referring to when He said, "do this in remembrance of Me"? He had just finished eating His last meal with His disciples before His death.

fellowship. He also wants you (us) to be a visible expression of who He is. This can only happen as you learn to live by *His* life instead of your *own* life. But *how* do you do that? How do you live by the life of an indwelling Lord? The first thing you must do is to receive that divine life. You must take that life within your spirit.

In the physical realm, how do you live by human life? You must first take the substance of life into your body. We call that substance, food. If you don't eat, you don't live. It's that simple. It's the same way in the spiritual realm. You must take Christ as your food in order to live by His life.

I'm not speaking of work here. Think about coming to the table to enjoy a meal. This is not work, this is enjoyment. Relax, take your time, and savor each morsel of food. Taste, *really* taste, all the different flavors brought on by the spices in every bite. Take your time and chew your food well. Take in each bite and receive that morsel as part of you. Feast upon the living Christ! This is not work. This is not study. This is not prayer in the conventional sense. This is dining upon and with your Lord. We are called, not only to dine *with* Him (fellowship); we are also called to dine *upon* Him (eating). He told us that He is the Bread of life. Just as He dines upon the Father and then lives by His life; so are we to dine upon Him and live by His life (John 6:57).

## Developing Habitual Fellowship

Turning to Christ as you eat is only one example of remembering Him and then turning to Him throughout the day. What we are talking about here is developing a habit; the habit of turning to your Lord who lives within you throughout the day. This is not a habit that is easy to

tunity to turn to Him. Do you realize how much "down-time" we all have everyday? I'm referring to times when we really aren't doing anything at all that demands our full attention. What about when you are waiting in line at the bank? What about when you are waiting in the lobby of the doctor's or dentist's office? Taking a shower. Warming up the car. Working out at the gym. Driving to pickup the kids from school. These are all times when you can turn to the temple within; enter the holy of holies and fellowship with the Lord of Glory!

Oh, there's one I forgot; turning the page to the next chapter in a book!

"When one knows how to stay near Him and remain in His presence, the presence of God knows how to melt and dissolve the hardness of the believer's heart. While the heart melts, it gives up a scent to God. That is why the Bridegroom, seeing that His Bride had melted in this way as soon as her Beloved had spoken, says to her: 'Who is the one who comes up from the desert like a little puff of perfume?'

"There is only one way to conquer your five senses, and that is by inward recollection. Or, to put it another way, the only way to conquer your five senses is by turning your soul completely inward to your spirit, there to possess a present God."

~ Jeanne Guyon ~

# Transformation

Transformation is one of the most misunderstood subjects in all of scripture. In our day it is definitely misunderstood by most believers and that is the reason why there is so little spiritual maturity found among us today. Just our *view* of transformation alone will determine how we live our "Christian" lives. The problem is that most Christians today have a twisted view of transformation. We all agree that God wants to transform us into His image, the problem arises in the question of *how*. How does God change us? Or *does* He even change us?

## The Improvement of the Old Man

The most common view of transformation today is that God is in the home improvement business. We are the house and He is the Contractor. Our house is a real mess. It's what you would call a "fixer upper." Beginning the day that we are saved, God begins His remodeling project to fix us up!

We are coworkers with Him in this project. So this

Christian in seven steps. The problem is that no one really tells us *how* to touch this Lord who lives within us. Your transformation does not depend upon you! It depends upon the life of God within you. Now, it is true that we must cooperate and yield to the dealings of the Holy Spirit upon our lives. But God is not interested in making us good people. He is not interested in a "home improvement" plan for the old man. He has crucified the old man on the cross! You have died and now your only life is hidden in Christ (see Col. 3:3; Romans 6; Gal. 2:20).

We must first ask ourselves; what is God's goal in transforming us into His image? Why does He desire to do this? What is His purpose in all of this? Without understanding His purpose and goal, we will never truly understand the "process" of transformation. Does God really change us? If so, *how* does He change us? And what part do we have to play in our transformation? Our fellowship with Him within our internal temple is a very important key to this transformation process. But first we must go back to the very beginning in order to see God's ultimate goal and purpose.

## The River of His Purpose

"Now a river flowed out of Eden to water the garden; and from there it divided and became four rivers. The name of the first is Pishon; it flows around the whole land of Havilah, where there is gold. And the gold of the land is good; the bdellium and the onyx stone are there." Genesis 2:10-12

One of the best ways to discover God's eternal purpose is to go back to the beginning of creation (before the

## Gold – the Divine Life

Gold always represents divinity in scripture; it represents God' life, in other words, God Himself. The gold referred to in Genesis chapter two is not the kind that needs to be refined by fire. It is *pure* gold that is naturally found as nuggets. This speaks of the life of Christ that the Father deposits into the spirit of every believer. As I have said many times in this book; you have the living Christ inside of you. You have pure gold inside of your spirit.

In the tabernacle of Moses, inside of the holy of holies, everything was covered with pure gold. All of the boards that held together that room were overlaid with gold. Gold was everywhere! This is how it is inside of your spirit. This place is filled with and covered in divine life. The ark is the place where God and man meet. The wood symbolizes humanity. The gold symbolizes divinity. They become one in the ark. They become one in Christ! We know that your spirit is the *real* holy of holies where you and God meet. As you fellowship with Him there, you partake more and more of His divine nature (2 Pet. 1:4). You cannot partake of His divine nature without being radically changed. The more you partake of Him, the more you are transformed into His image.

Another example of this is in the eating of bread. You know that Christ is the true Bread of life. You have Bread living inside of your spirit. But are you *eating* this bread? There is an old saying; "you are what you eat." Are you eating of Christ? Do you take *Him* as your daily Bread? All true Spirit born believers have the Bread living inside of them. But very few actually eat that Bread! It's only by *eating* that you are transformed. Now please be clear as to

## God is in the Building Business

The whole of scripture is the history and record of God's building. In the beginning we see the garden containing the raw materials needed for this building. At the end, we see the city that God has built with the gold, the precious stones, and the pearls. Of course, these things are all a picture of Christ and the church, the real building of God. You *are* His building! He is in the process of transforming us into precious stones and building us together.

## Two Ways that God Uses to Transform Us

The first way is exactly what I am sharing in this book; our fellowship with God. We are changed from glory to glory by beholding Him, and loving Him, and sharing His life. The more that we meet with Him, spirit to Spirit, the more that we are transformed into His image. Isn't this amazing? We are transformed from rocks into precious stones simply by being with Him!

The first step in the transformation of the diamond is that the carbon must be buried deep into the earth. You have been placed deep into Christ. But now you must *abide* in Him! Being in Him is your *position*, abiding in Him is your *activity*. Every time that you turn to Him and abide in Him you are being transformed. Even though you may not "feel" anything or even sense His presence, if you turn to Him in faith, He is doing His work of transformation in you by the Holy Spirit.

The second step in the transformation process is the application of pressure and suffering. This is the application of His cross. He uses relationships with other people

"What, then, is this spiritual house? What is this Church? Let us not have an objective mentality about this, thinking of it as something somewhere outside of and apart from ourselves. What is it? The answer is a very simple one. The spiritual house of God is Christ Himself. Yes, but not Christ personally alone, but Christ in you, in me, the hope of glory. Oh, it is just here that all the mistakes have been made about the Church, with such disastrous results. The Church, the House of God, is simply Christ Himself in undivided oneness found in all those in whom He really dwells. That is all. That is the Church. Seek to root out of your mentality any and every other idea of the Church. It is not Christ divided into a thousand or a million fragments amongst so many believers. It is still one Christ. You and I are not the Church. It is Christ in you and in me that is the Church."

~ T. Austin-Sparks ~

# The Corporate Temple

As I stated in the introduction of this book, your fellowship with God is not just an individual matter. It is extremely important that you realize that everything I have shared in this book is to be understood in the context of the corporate body of Christ. We learn to know Him *together*. You get to know Him individually and personally, but you also get to know Him together with the saints. Paul spoke about both of these relationships in his letters.

"Or do you not know that your body is a temple of the Holy Spirit who is in you . . ." I Cor. 6:19

This is speaking to the individual believer. You are a temple because the living God (by His Spirit) dwells within you.

"For *we* are the temple of the living God; just as God said, 'I will dwell in *them* and walk among *them*; and I will be *their* God, and *they* shall be my people . . .'"
II Cor. 6:16

We will not see the return of true church life to this earth again in any major way until we learn to live by the life of Christ within us together as His body. This book is not about you as an individual becoming a spiritual giant. The purpose of this book is for you to learn how to cooperate with the divine life that God has placed within you so that *He* will get what *He* wants. The goal is that God will have His holy temple, His bride, His body, His New Jerusalem that will expand the expression of His glorious Son! Yes, He wants you to grow in your individual sonship as well, but that is only part of the story. The *fullness* of Christ can only be expressed through the body. (Eph. 1:23)

**The Expression of the Godhead**

In an earlier chapter I shared about the fellowship of the Godhead. This is the relationship and activity going on between the Father, Son, and Holy Spirit in the spiritual realm. What is vitally important is that you understand in your spirit that God wants to express that fellowship in a visible way in *this* realm. In fact, He wants to express that relationship and fellowship through the church! In fact, the fellowship of the Godhead is the basis and foundation for all church life. If you want to learn how the church lives and functions then you need to see the fellowship going on inside of God Himself. This is the model for the church. This is where church life began!

When God created man He said, "Let *Us* make man in *Our* image, in *Our* likeness . . ." (Gen. 1:26). He used corporate language here (Us, Our) because He was creating a *corporate* image. Since God is corporate (three Persons in one), it stands to reason that His image would also need

this was an invitation to partake of His fellowship. God wanted to become *one* with man. This oneness would take place within His fellowship with man. He wanted man to be a community just as He is a community. This could only happen if man chose to receive God's life within him. This choice was represented by the tree of life.

Of course, we know that man chose knowledge instead of life. Jesus Christ came as the true Tree of Life to fulfill God's purpose for man. He was the Grain of Wheat that was crushed and fell into the ground so that the Seed would be multiplied. Now, through resurrection, God's life could be placed in many individuals who would make up the one loaf. God's plan to expand His community could now be realized.

## God's Heart for Community

True church life is the spiritual and practical expression of the fellowship of the Godhead. The fullness of the Godhead is contained within Christ and Christ lives inside of you! That wonderful flow of divine fellowship within the Godhead is happening right now inside of your spirit! The Father, Son and Holy Spirit are sharing their love, life and communication with one another inside of you right now. This fellowship is meant to flow out of you to others in the body of Christ. The life must flow out. As you share this fellowship with other believers and divine life is exchanged between the members of the body, something wonderful is born on this earth; community! This is God's heart. This is God's passion.

This cannot be accomplished by you as a separated, isolated individual. God's image can only be realized by a

abodes. You are an abode and I am an abode. Every Spirit-born believer is an abode of the Holy Spirit, but yet, in our Father's house there are *many* abodes! We are an abode for God and He is an abode for us. *You* are a temple and *we* are a temple. This is not just a spiritual reality, but a practical one.

Your fellowship with God should not only be an individual experience, it should be corporate. You should be learning to know Him and experience Him *together* with other believers in your local area. You should definitely be sharing the Lord together with others on a regular, if not daily, basis. Your spiritual nourishment will not only come from Christ directly through the Spirit, but also through His body. You need others to help you see the full and well rounded Christ. By yourself, you will come to have a "lop-sided" view of Him. You need your brothers and sisters to give you the complete picture.

Many believers contact me either through email or the phone wanting to know what they should do about meeting together with other believers. They have left the organized "church" system and don't know what to do. They want to know Christ in a deeper way and to experience true first century style church life but they have no such body of believers near them. Perhaps, you dear reader, are in that same situation. I will tell you what I have told all the others.

You really only have two choices. One choice is to really get serious in prayer and ask God to bring other like-minded believers together in your area. The other choice is to move to an area where there is already an established fellowship of believers.

"Begin seeing Christ behind everything. When you finally understand that Christ is everything you need, then you will have become truly Christocentric. Then will you share with the Father the most precious thing He has – His Son. Christ will become your only perspective, your only hope, your only possession and your only interest. Everything else will fade into insignificance."

~ Manfred R. Haller ~

# The Centrality of Christ

## Who is the Center of the Universe?

We, by and large, are not a Christ centered people. Christ is not our only focus, prospective, and goal. He is not our everything, our life, our all. Everything in our lives does *not* revolve around Him and His purpose. You can say that He is *in* your life, but can you honestly say that He *is* your life? Can you honestly say that He is the sum total of all your hopes, dreams, wishes, and goals? Can you honestly say that He is at the very heart of all your thoughts, actions, and plans? Is He the very breath you take, and the reason you get up out of bed every morning? Are you passionately obsessed with this One whom you call Lord?

We have a Christianity today that is dangerously close to becoming Christ-less! We say that He is the Center and Life, but in reality, *we* are the center of the universe we live in. Beginning with our "gospel" and all the way up to our "ministry," it is all geared up to serve man and the needs of man. Christ is not the focal point. Man is the focal point.

for *our lives*. Christians are always asking, "What is the will of God for *my life*?" Here again, we are at the center. Now what you need to understand is that the will of God for your life should be an outgrowth of the eternal purpose of God. In other words, God's eternal purpose should be the determining factor in discovering His will for your personal life. All of His desires for your life will be in direct relationship to His eternal purpose. If you come in line with His purpose, then all of the details in your own life will just naturally fall in place.

God has a purpose. God has had something in His mind and in His heart from before the foundation of the world. In fact, this purpose was the motivating factor in Him creating the visible and invisible realms. The purpose is His sole obsession, His only passion, His reason for doing *everything* that He does. All of His words and all of His actions tie together to flow into this one great river of His purpose. *Nothing* is more important to Him than this and He is really blind to all else. All lesser things fall by the wayside in His thoughts and in His works. His eye and His mind are singular in their focus upon this one purpose. He *never* deviates even one inch to the left or to the right of this one singular purpose. His eye is fixed and His thought is focused and they are never removed from His one goal for even one instant. Nothing else ever crosses His mind and nothing else ever distracts His attention. In fact, if it be known, He even eats, drinks, and breathes this one great purpose. This purpose is a great mystery and secret to most of the sons and daughters of men. But to those who draw close to Him; to those who really want to know Him and love Him; and give up their lives for Him; to those He will reveal His heart.

moment! How could we ever allow ourselves to be pulled away by lesser things? Dear reader, you and I have been called according to this wonderful purpose. In light of this knowledge, let us so order everything in our lives to line up with this one great purpose. Let *this* be the reason why we do everything that we do. Let *this* be the reason why we get out of bed every morning. Let *this* be the reason we take every breath. Let *this* be our sole passion, and sole obsession. For we have died, and our lives are hidden with Christ in God. And *Christ* is now our only life.

The Father wants to express and increase His Son in all His glorious fullness. He is doing this through the church, one member at a time. As you learn to see with His perspective and think with *His* thoughts, the more you will become a Christ "obsessed" person. The more that you eat and drink of Him, the more that you will be able to express Him. The more that you eat of the Tree of Life, the more that you become a part of that tree by becoming a branch. This happens by abiding in Him. This is what I have been sharing with you in this book.

## To You or For You?

"And He put all things in subjection under His feet, and gave Him as head over all things *to the church*, which is His body, the fullness of Him who fills all in all." Eph. 1:22-23

Paul tells us in this passage that the Father gave Christ as head over *all* things *to the church*. My question to you is this; is He all things *to* you or is He all things *for* you? The difference is monumental. In these two little

center?  Christ is many things for you, but what is He *to* you?  Contrary to popular belief, Jesus Christ does not exist for us!  He lives and breathes to please and glorify the Father.  He lives to fulfill God's purpose.  When you become a truly Christ centered person, He will occupy all your thoughts and your conversations.  You won't want to talk about yourself, or the weather, or politics.  You will want to share the sightings you have had of your glorious Lord!

## How Big is Your Christ?

When you first turned to Christ you took Him as your Savior.  Isn't it odd how we take Him as our Savior but we do not take Him as our Salvation?  Rather, the way that it is presented to us (by preachers) is that He is the Savior, but He gives us this "thing" called salvation.  So we receive Him as the Giver, but not as the gift.  Salvation is something that is separate from the Savior.  Now, since He has given us this thing called salvation, we own it.  It is now something which we possess just as if I gave you a present for your birthday.  Do you see how everything becomes twisted to be about us?

Christ doesn't give you salvation.  He *is* Salvation!  You must receive *Him* as your Salvation.

"But by *His* doing you are in Christ Jesus, who became to us wisdom from God, and righteousness, and sanctification, and redemption . . ." I Cor. 1:30

This is just one example of how we make it all about us.  Of course, there is nothing new about this.  When the Lord walked this earth as a man, we can clearly see this

the water represents His life and that nothing can stop that life from flowing. His life is not dependant upon outward circumstances or the surrounding environment. Hardness and dryness could not stop the flow of His life.

But then Paul says something which is absolutely outrageous. That *rock* was also Christ! Notice with me that he does not only tell us that the water was Christ (spiritual drink), but that the *rock* itself was also Christ!

My dear reader, do you sometimes find yourself in a desert with nothing to drink? When you look around, what do you see? Do you see sand, and dry brush and rocks? Or do you see Christ? To find Him, look for the driest and hardest place. Instead of looking for a way out of the desert, look for a rock! He is already there, where you are, but He is in the most unlikely place. He is in the driest and hardest place. In fact, He *is* the driest and hardest place! He *is* the rock.

Of course, we always look for the water first. By nature, we are people looking for a "quick fix." We are looking for an oasis with water just bubbling out of the ground. But the water is found inside of a rock. The water is found inside of the driest and hardest of all places – inside of solid rock. Take Him as your Rock. Take Him as your hard place. Don't try to just receive what the rock gives (water), but receive the *Rock* Himself. See that hard (difficult) place that you are in for what it is – Christ! Is it possible to turn rocks into diamonds? Yes, if you will take Christ as your Rock and drink the water of life from Him.

**Take Him as Your All**

The rock is just one example of how we receive Christ as our All. If you look at the gospel of John you will

". . . that He would grant you, according to the riches of His glory, to be strengthened with power through His Spirit in the inner man; so that Christ may dwell in your hearts through faith; and that you, being rooted and grounded in love, may be able to comprehend with all the saints what is the breadth and length and height and depth, and to know the love of Christ which surpasses knowledge, that you may be filled up to all the fullness of God."

~ Paul of Tarsus ~

# The Exploration of Christ

My wife and I live in the beautiful state of Colorado, U.S.A. There is a place which is about two hours away from us called Glenwood Springs that is a well known resort area because of the natural hot springs and vapor caves that people come to enjoy. The town is in a canyon located right by the Colorado River with mountains all around. One of those mountains contains natural caverns or caves that have been made into a tour for people to explore. One day, we went on this cavern tour.

We rode up to the top of the mountain on one of those aerial tram rides. When we arrived at the top, we bought our tour ticket and then waited for the next tour. After our group had assembled, our tour guide took us deep into the mountain to explore the caves. The air was so cool and still down there and we saw many things that we had never seen before. We marveled at the stalactites and sta-lagmites, the large pinnacle shaped rock formations that shot down from the ceiling and up from the floor. Many of these spots on the ceiling were dripping wet releasing water

every turn there are new passage ways to be uncovered. Around every corner there are whole new worlds to be pursued. This territory has been uncharted and you and I have been called to the frontier of this never ending country.

## Cave Expressions

As we walked along through the caverns our tour guide would point out certain interesting items. There were many rock formations, stalactites, and stalagmites that the "cavers" had named because they looked like other things that they could relate to. For example, there was one stalactite that had the shape of an Oscar, the award that is given to people in the movie industry at the academy of awards presentation. It was dubbed "Oscar", of course. There was another one that looked like the Grinch in the Dr. Seuss story of "How the Grinch Stole Christmas." Of course, it was named, the "Grinch." And there were many other such items. It was as if the cave was making shapes that we could relate to -- almost as if the cave was trying to express itself to us in a way that we could understand.

Paul told us that Christ is the image of the invisible God. The God of the universe wanted to express Himself; He wanted to be made visible. Christ is the visible expression of an invisible God. How can this be? This is made possible because Christ is both God and Man. He is both humanity and divinity in the same body. But please understand something here. When Paul speaks of Christ being the image of God, he is not only referring to a man (the person), Jesus Christ. He is speaking of the corporate Christ. He is speaking of the Head and the Body, the one *new* Man! Please realize with me that the Head and the

inside of it was a miniature replica of the cave itself. If you could shrink yourself down small enough, you could enter this "colony" and it would look a lot like the large cave you had just left! Can you image it? A cave within a cave, but this cave is alive! And these "colonies" were located all throughout the cave. Caves within caves. Colonies within caves. Oh, the wonder of it all! This just boggled my mind; however, it did not surprise me. The scriptures tell us that all of creation speaks of Him.

## The Colonies of Heaven

There are many such colonies within Christ. There are colonies or "outposts" of His kingdom. These "clusters" of saints are the local, geographical expression of Christ Himself. They are miniature cities that are made up of living stones. They stand on the ground of the one large city of God; the New Jerusalem. They are all part of the one large city, and yet each one is a mini replica of that same city. When you enter into one of these "colonies," you sense that you have just entered into the New Jerusalem. God and man have become one. The life of God is the food and the Spirit of God is the drink in that city. God Himself is the light and the Lamb is the lamp that contains the light of that great city.

These colonies are separate expressions yet they are all one with the cave and one with each other. They are all made of the same material and live by the same life. The cave itself is what sustains them and their lifeblood is drawn from its walls. Since the cave and the colonies are one, there is no end to the depths of the riches found within

are without end and have no measure, eternal worlds within eternal worlds, heavens within heavens; all of this (and more) is inside of your Lord! These heavenly places are *in* Christ. There are unsearchable riches and unfathomable depths within Him. All of the fullness of deity dwells within Him. All of the fullness of the Godhead dwells within Him. All of the power, authority, and character of God dwells within Him. The river of life, the tree of life, and the throne of God all dwell within Him. All of the precious stones, the gold, and the pearls that have been transformed out of clay dwell within Him. The tabernacle and temple of God dwell within Him. The holy of holies which contains the manna, the rod that budded, and the tablets of the law dwell within Him. And don't forget one other thing . . . *YOU* also dwell inside of Him!

And this glorious Lord, this One who is the sum of all spiritual things and all spiritual blessings, this same Lord dwells within YOU!

So what are you waiting for? Let the expedition begin!

# Recommended Reading

*A Testament of Devotion* . . . . . . . . . . . . . . Thomas Kelley

*Experiencing the Depths of Jesus Christ* . . . Jeanne Guyon

*In Christ* . . . . . . . . . . . . . . . . . . . . . . . . . T. Austin Sparks

*Living with Jesus Today* . . . . . . . . . . . . . Juan Carlos Ortiz

*Practicing His Presence* . . . . . . . . . . . . Brother Lawrence

*The Divine Romance* . . . . . . . . . . . . . . . . . . Gene Edwards

*The Glorious Church* . . . . . . . . . . . . . . . . Watchman Nee

*The Highest Life* . . . . . . . . . . . . . . . . . . . . Gene Edwards

*The Interior Castle* . . . . . . . . . . . . . . . . . Theresa of Avila

*The Interior Way* . . . . . . . . . . . . . . . . . . . . Jeanne Guyon

*The Mystery of God* . . . . . . . . . . . . . . . . . Manfred Haller

*The Normal Christian Life* . . . . . . . . . . . . Watchman Nee

*The Secret to the Christian Life* . . . . . . . . . . Gene Edwards

*The Seeking Heart* . . . . . . . . . . . . . . . . . Francois Fenelon

*The Spiritual Guide* . . . . . . . . . . . . . . . . . Michael Molinos

**Other books by Milt Rodriguez**

*The Coat of Many Colors*

*The Priesthood of All Believers*

Visit our website at:

www.therebuilders.org

**Published by The Rebuilders**

2177 S. Grand Mesa Dr.

Cedaredge, CO  81413

970-856-6492